CATHERINE
DE MEDICI
THE POWER BEHIND THE FRENCH THRONE

CATHERINE
DE MEDICI
THE POWER BEHIND THE FRENCH THRONE

by Barbara A. Somervill

Content Adviser: Katherine Crawford, Ph.D.,
Assistant Professor, Department of History,
Vanderbilt University

Reading Adviser: Susan Kesselring, M.A.,
Literacy Educator, Rosemount–Apple Valley–
Eagan (Minnesota) School District

COMPASS POINT BOOKS MINNEAPOLIS, MINNESOTA

Compass Point Books
3109 West 50th Street, #115
Minneapolis, MN 55410

Visit Compass Point Books on the Internet at *www.compasspointbooks.com*
or e-mail your request to *custserv@compasspointbooks.com*

Editor: Jennifer VanVoorst
Page Production: Heather Griffin
Photo Researcher: Svetlana Zhurkin
Cartographer: XNR Productions, Inc.
Library Consultant: Kathleen Baxter

Art Director: Jaime Martens
Creative Director: Keith Griffin
Editorial Director: Carol Jones
Managing Editor: Catherine Neitge

Library of Congress Cataloging-in-Publication Data
Somervill, Barbara A.
  Catherine de Medici : the power behind the French throne / by Barbara
A. Somervill.
    p. cm. — (Signature lives)
  Includes bibliographical references and index.
  ISBN 0-7565-1581-5 (hardcover)
  1. Catherine de Médicis, Queen, consort of Henry II, King of France,
1519–1589—Juvenile literature. 2. Queens—France—Biography—
Juvenile literature. 3. Mothers of kings and rulers—France—Biography—
Juvenile literature. 4. France—History—16th century—Juvenile literature.
5. Reformation—France—History—16th century—Juvenile literature. I.
Title. II. Series.
  DC119.8.S69 2005
  944'.028092—dc22   2005027111

Table of Contents

1 THE ST. BARTHOLOMEW'S DAY MASSACRE

Chapter

❦

The hired killer sat in a window overlooking a narrow Paris street. He had been waiting for his victim to stroll past. Now, as Admiral Gaspard de Coligny came into view, the assassin took aim. Just as he shot, however, Coligny bent to fix his shoe. The bullet struck Coligny's arm. He was severely wounded, but he wasn't dead—at least not yet. If the wound became infected, he might lose the arm or even die.

Catherine de Medici had arranged the assassination. According to her, France's biggest problem in 1572 was Admiral de Coligny. He was simply too powerful, too dangerous, and too Protestant. Catherine's son, 22-year-old Charles IX, was king of France, but he was weak, wishy-washy, and easily fooled by those around him. Having lost his father

Admiral Coligny's assassination turned into a murderous free-for-all, as Parisian Catholics turned on their Protestant fellow citizens in the St. Bartholomew's Day Massacre.

Admiral de Coligny was a Huguenot leader and onetime friend of Catherine de Medici.

at age 9, he now looked to Coligny as a father figure. This concerned Catherine.

Catherine believed that Admiral Coligny threatened the Roman Catholic Church, her son's rule, and most importantly, her own power. She had taken action to remove the threat by hiring an assassin, but when that plan failed, she refused to give up.

Catherine had gone too far not to finish what she had started. This time, Catherine drew her son, the king, into the assassination plot. She started a rumor that Admiral Coligny was planning a military campaign against the king. When Charles learned of Coligny's alleged plans, he shouted in a fit of rage, "Then kill them all. Kill them all." He drew up a list of leading court Protestants, including Coligny, to be assassinated.

Paris in the late 1500s was a city divided along religious lines, but 1572 had brought Protestants hope of a reconciliation. That August, French Protestants, called Huguenots, had flocked to the city for the marriage of their leader, Henri, King of Navarre, to Princess Marguerite de Valois, Catherine's youngest daughter. On the city streets, the Huguenots' stark black-and-white outfits identified them as Protestants.

But Paris was Catholic to its core. The presence of so many Protestants brought Catholic

The Huguenots were the French branch of the Protestant Reformation. In France, John Calvin organized his version of the Reformation. He fled France for Geneva, Switzerland, where he converted many Catholics to the Protestant faith. Calvin's followers were called Huguenots. The name Huguenots came from the word hugeon, meaning people who walk at night. This referred to the night services forced on Protestants by Catholics.

tempers to the boiling point. To protect themselves against attack, many of the Huguenots began carrying weapons. Catholics did the same. They quickly collected weapons to protect themselves from a feared Protestant uprising. Petty squabbles broke out on Paris streets. Tempers flared, and mobs roamed the streets looking for victims to beat up.

Catherine recognized that trouble was brewing, but she was not a very religious person and did not understand the fanatical views of the time. She did not understand that Parisian Catholics—and indeed French Catholics generally—had grown enraged to the point of murderous fury against the Protestants. Coligny's failed assassination had only fueled the fires of distrust between French Protestants and Catholics. Still, few could have expected what happened next.

At 3 A.M. on St. Bartholomew's Day—Sunday, August 24, 1572—the bells of Paris' Hall of Justice rang out. The king's Swiss guard marched to the hotel where Admiral Coligny was staying. Coligny's bodyguard unlocked the door and was stabbed. Coligny took a sword to the chest before being thrown out the window to the street below.

Members of the king's guard began killing the Huguenots staying at the Louvre, the king's palace. Guards herded the Huguenots into the courtyard. The guards struck down the men with swords or shot them with arrows. Women and children, still

The violence in the Paris streets was savage and unrestrained.

dressed in their nightshirts, watched their husbands and fathers die before their eyes.

Catherine de Medici and her son, the king, rid France of its Huguenot leaders in under two hours, but the killing continued. King Charles IX ordered people to return peace to Paris' streets. The crowds, however, ignored his orders. Mobs poured through the streets, and violence continued.

On the city streets, Catholic Parisians attacked Huguenots. Men and women lay bleeding in the middle of the road. Their throats were cut and their bodies mutilated. Thieves stole goods off the bodies of the dead, and mobs hurled baskets with dead and dying Huguenot children into the Seine River.

The massacre gave people a chance to rid themselves of enemies—and not just Protestants. Debtors killed the people they owed, wiping out their debts instantly. Husbands rid themselves of unwanted wives. Jealous lovers killed their rivals. People burned books, houses, and public buildings. They stole goods from shops and robbed homes. There was no limit to the violence.

Afterward, no one knew the whole truth. Rumors spread that the Huguenots started the fighting. Those Huguenots who survived fled Paris. But much of the blame for the massacre fell to Catherine herself, thus justifying an already sinister reputation and earning her many nicknames: the Black Queen, the Sinister Queen, the Maggot from Italy's Tomb, and Madame La Serpente (Madame Snake).

Catherine, however, remained as flexible and capable as she'd been before the massacre. In an age of religious idealism, Catherine had always been practical. Though her actions may have led to murder in the streets, she needed to put that unfortunate outcome aside and consider how to keep Charles IX on the throne and avoid more problems.

Catherine's reign—first as queen and then as queen mother—was marked by a single-minded devotion to maintaining her family's rule. Still, it was Catherine herself who was the true power behind the French throne. Despite a seemingly endless succession of personal tragedies, Catherine still managed to leave a greater mark on history than her pompous father-in-law, her unfaithful husband, or her weakling sons. Though they were kings, the men in her life were no match for the determined queen, Catherine de Medici. ℘

Catherine de Medici was a powerful and controversial French leader.

2 AN ORPHAN DAUGHTER

❧⟨∞⟩❧

Catherine de Medici's story began in Florence, Italy. Italy's map in the 1500s was very different from today's map. Renaissance Italy was a cluster of small republics or city-states, such as Genoa, Milan, Parma, and Florence. Spain ruled large chunks of Italy— Corsica, Sicily, and most of the southern peninsula, while the pope and the Catholic Church governed Rome and the Papal States.

The major powers in Europe during this time included France, Spain, the Catholic Church (Rome), and the Holy Roman Empire. Desire for greater power and riches created enemies and allies among the major powers. France, Spain, and the Holy Roman Empire struggled for domination of Europe, and Italy was the battleground. Because of their small

King Francois I of France, seeking to extend his kingdom, proposed the marriage that led to Catherine's birth.

Within the map:

SWISS CONFED.

TYROL

CARNIOLA

Holy Roman Empire
Map shows boundaries of 1500.

Duchy of Milan

Duchy of Savoy

Venice

KINGDOM OF HUNGARY

KINGDOM OF FRANCE

Piacenza

Parma

Reggio

Modena

Duchy of Urbino

REPUBLIC OF VENICE

OTTOMAN EMPIRE

Pisa

Florence

Leghorn

Florence

Rep. of Siena

REPUBLIC OF GENOA

PAPAL STATES

Adriatic Sea

N W E S

Corsica

Rome

KINGDOM OF NAPLES

Sardinia

Tyrrhenian Sea

Ionian Sea

KINGDOM OF ARAGON

Mediterranean Sea

Sicily

0   100 miles

0   100 kilometers

During the 1500s, Italy was divided into small republics and city-states.

size, city-states were easy prey for European leaders, and short-lived wars shifted bits of Italy from one country's ownership to another.

Like the rest of the European leaders, France's King Francois I wanted a piece of Italy for his empire. When war didn't work, the king decided to use marriage to gain power in Italy.

Francois I found the perfect husband for one of his female relatives: Lorenzo II de Medici, Duke of Urbino and grandson of renowned arts patron Lorenzo the Magnificent. In 1516, Lorenzo II became the leader of the Florentine republic. He was 34 years old and unmarried.

King Francois wrote to congratulate Lorenzo on his new power. He told the new ruler:

> I intend to help you with all my power. I also wish to marry you off to some beautiful and good lady of noble birth and of my kin, so that the love which I bear you may grow and be strengthened.

The Medicis of Florence were a powerful, wealthy family of merchants. During the reign of Lorenzo the Magnificent, the family supported such famous artists as Raphael, Leonardo da Vinci, and Michelangelo. By the 1500s, the family's power was weakening, but the Medici family motto, "Le Temps Revient" ("Our Time Will Return") would soon be realized as Catherine de Medici rose to power in France.

This attention from a king bolstered Lorenzo's ego. His family was wealthy, but they were still commoners. Marrying a member of a royal family— no matter how distant from the throne—was an honor Lorenzo could not pass up. The bride who was being offered was Madeleine de la Tour d'Auvergne, then just 16 years old.

Lorenzo and Madeleine wed on April 25, 1518, in

Lorenzo II de Medici was part of a wealthy family with merchant roots.

Amboise, France. King Francois gave them a royal wedding. Celebrations ran for days with mock battles, jousting, dancing, and feasting. Lorenzo offered rich

gifts to France's nobility. The bride received 10,000 gold coins called *écus*. Little did the bride and groom realize that they would not live long enough to enjoy their gifts.

By the time the new couple returned to Florence, Lorenzo was dying. Historians believe he suffered from both syphilis and tuberculosis. Young and pregnant, Madeleine stayed in Florence while her new husband went to the mountains for his health.

On April 13, 1519, Madeleine gave birth to a girl she named Caterina Maria Romola de Medici. The baby was healthy enough, but she was a disappointment to her dying father. He knew there would be no more chances to produce a son, an heir to the Medici fortunes.

Though they are rarely found today, in past times diseases such as syphilis and tuberculosis were common. Syphilis is a disease caused by bacteria that attacks the brain, internal organs, nerves, eyes, heart, and joints. Tuberculosis, also a bacterial disease, attacks the lungs, leaving its victims weak. In its final stage, victims cough desperately, often coughing up blood. Today, most ancient diseases can be cured with antibiotics, but since antibiotics didn't exist in the 1500s, victims usually died.

Madeleine never recovered from childbirth and died two weeks later. On May 4, 1519, Lorenzo died as well. Not even a month old, the girl the Florentines fondly called the duchessina was left an orphan.

King Francois I asked to raise the child in France, but Caterina's great-uncle, Pope Leo X, had a different idea. Caterina went to Rome to be cared for by her grandmother, Alfonsina Orsini. More tragedy was to come, however. Alfonsina died within a year, and once again Caterina had no one to care for her.

"She comes bearing the calamities of the Greeks!" Pope Leo X cried on seeing her. He arranged for Caterina to be raised by her aunt, Clarissa Strozzi. The Strozzi house was lively, and Caterina enjoyed playing with her many cousins. But this arrangement was short-lived. Pope Leo X died in 1521, and 3-year-old Caterina moved back to Florence with a distant relative, Cardinal Giulio de Medici.

Two years later, the Catholic Church named Cardinal Giulio de Medici pope. He chose the name Clement VII. The pope left to live in Rome, and Caterina went to live in a series of convent schools.

The city of Florence was filled with beautiful waterways, churches, and homes.

Nuns often took care of daughters from wealthy families. Caterina grew up small and thin, with the pop-eyes typical of the Medici family. She was charming, with good manners and a strong mind. For a girl, she was extremely well educated, fond of art, music, and architecture.

By the late 1520s, Pope Clement VII and the Holy Roman Emperor, Charles V, were at odds. In 1529, after spending two years wreaking havoc in Rome, Charles' army headed into Italy and laid siege to the city of Florence.

For nearly a year, Caterina's convent, the Medici palaces, and Florence's common folk suffered together. No food or goods came into the city. By the time the siege was finally lifted, Caterina was 11 years old. She had begun wearing a nun's habit and cutting her hair short. She planned to become a nun. But Clement VII had other ideas for Caterina.

> *During the siege of Florence, the Florentine sculptor and painter Michelangelo served the city as a military engineer. In his role as "governor and procurator general for the defense of Florence," he protected citizens during the siege by designing fortifications and walls to be built around the city.*

Since her birth, Caterina's eventual marriage had been the object of much discussion. She was too valuable as a political bargaining chip to be allowed the quiet life of a nun. The pope needed an ally to help him protect the church's Italian properties from

Catherine's relative, Giulio de Medici, became Pope Clement VII in 1523.

Emperor Charles V, and Caterina was the central figure in his international policy. So in 1530, Caterina left the convent for Rome. There, she lived at the Palazzo Medici under the care of her great-aunt

Lucrezia Salviati. Caterina watched as the ruined city was rebuilt, and continued to nurture her interest in art and architecture. She also learned Greek and Latin and studied mathematics, a subject at which she was particularly adept. And of course, she continued to develop the skills and qualities needed to make an important marriage.

In 1531, France's King Francois wrote to Pope Clement suggesting a match between his second son, Henri de Valois, Duke of Orleans, and Caterina de Medici, Duchess of Urbino. Clement was excited at the political advantages the marriage would provide him and called it "the greatest match in the world." The pope might have been surprised to learn that at the same time Caterina was emerging from the siege at her Italian convent, Henri was emerging from imprisonment in a Spanish court.

King Francois had great ambitions and poor military skills. Several years earlier, he had been taken prisoner in the Battle of Pavia. After signing a treaty to end the conflict, he bargained for his own release. The king offered his two sons, Dauphin Francois

The Holy Roman Empire, based in German-speaking areas of central Europe, existed for nearly a millennium—from 962 to 1806. It was closely associated with the Roman Catholic Church. Emperor Charles V was the most powerful European leader since Charlemagne, but by the end of the 16th century, the empire had fallen into decline as religious differences split the empire and lesser kings and dukes asserted their independence.

and Henri, as hostages against his fulfilling his side of the treaty. King Francois left his sons captive in Spain for more than four years. Henri was 6 when he was handed over to Spain, and nearly 11 when he was freed.

In 1525, King Francois I of France was defeated in the Battle of Pavia, leading to his sons' captivity in Spain.

In 1531, the Italian pope and the French king signed a preliminary marriage agreement that scheduled Caterina and Henri to be wed in the summer of 1533. King Francois wanted his son's bride to move to France right away, but Pope Clement

was not willing to give her up so quickly.

A young woman like Caterina grew up expecting that her hand in marriage would be sold to the highest bidder. Romance mattered little when weighed against land and power. But among the wealthy and powerful, the bride and groom were often the last to learn of their proposed marriage. And so Caterina—called Catherine from this point—only learned that she was to be married and to whom when she started learning French. ❧

Young Caterina de Medici

3 A LIFE AT COURT

⟡

In July 1533, Catherine received a gift of jewels from her soon-to-be father-in-law, King Francois I. Pope Clement VII gave her a dowry of 100,000 gold coins, plus another 30,000 for giving up her share of the Medici estate. In addition, Catherine's dowry would include the Italian cities of Pisa, Leghorn, Reggio, Modena, Parma, and Piacenza. The money was handy, but the foothold in Italy was Francois' real reason for agreeing to the marriage.

For her trip to France, Catherine packed a king's ransom in gold and jewels. She added cloth of silver and gold, silks, and velvets to her belongings. She brought black silk bed sheets, a gold belt covered with rubies and diamonds, and some extremely large pearls. Catherine's bridal finery was so sumptuous

Italian commoner Catherine de Medici and French Prince Henri de Valois were wed on October 28, 1533.

When Catherine de Medici arrived for her wedding she wore teardrop-shaped pearl earrings. More than 20 years later, her son married Mary Stuart, Queen of Scots, and Catherine gave the earrings to Mary. Some years after that, Queen Elizabeth I of England had Mary Stuart beheaded. Not wanting the earrings to go to waste, Elizabeth took them for herself. Many portraits of Queen Elizabeth feature Catherine de Medici's pearl earrings.

and costly that the Duke of Florence levied a tax on the Florentine people that, though he claimed it was to reinforce the city's defenses, was actually to pay for Catherine's bridalwear.

King Francois and his court met Catherine, Pope Clement VII, and the Medici party in Marseille, France. Francois arranged for the wedding party to live in two palaces across from each other. The road between the palaces was turned into a hall for the wedding.

The pope and the king signed the marriage contracts, and the next day, October 28, Catherine married Henri de Valois, Duke of Orleans. The bride and groom were only 14.

Catherine joined the French royal household as the new Duchess of Orleans. Her new father-in-law had been king of France for 18 years when Catherine married Henri. Her new mother-in-law, Queen Eleanor, was Francois' second wife, a woman the king disliked immensely. His first wife, Claude, had died in 1524 after providing France with four royal children—three sons and a daughter. The dauphin, Francois, was the oldest, followed by

Henri, Charles, and Marguerite.

Catherine tried hard to fit in, but Henri had little interest in her. Luckily, King Francois saw great promise in his new daughter-in-law. He loved to hunt, and Catherine was an able rider. She introduced the sidesaddle to France. The sidesaddle was a great improvement over the *sambue* platforms that forced women to ride sideways with no control over their horses. Catherine also had excellent manners and showed a keen interest in geography, physics, and astronomy. These were topics that drew Francois' interest.

Horses were given special training if they were to carry a lady.

Francois I's court was a moving city as it

traveled from castle to castle throughout the country. At times, nearly 10,000 people attended the court, along with 18,000 horses and enough wagons to haul food, belongings, clothing, and furniture. Wagons carried the bedding, chairs, tables, plates, utensils, pots, pans, and spices from one place to the next. Nobles, gentlewomen, and gentlemen rode on horseback, while their servants walked.

Castle kitchens fed several thousand people at least twice a day. Hunts provided whatever meat they could, added to calves, lambs, and poultry that were butchered. Fruit, vegetables, and grains disappeared from local orchards and fields, leaving little for the

Hunting was one of the ways of providing food for traveling courts in the 1500s.

folks left behind. Local people were glad to see the royal party leave.

Removal to the next castle was driven by food and fuel—and smell. By the time food and fuel became scarce, the castle latrines were full of human waste. The stench was horrendous. The castle's goods were quickly packed, and the king and his party moved on. This constant movement throughout the kingdom was called a progress.

While the king progressed from castle to castle, his kingdom was being torn in two by religious differences. Beginning in 1517, when a German priest named Martin Luther nailed his demands for reform to the door of the church in Wittenberg, Germany, small groups of reformers had begun protesting church practices. Because they were protesting Catholic practices and seeking to reform the church, their growing movement came to be known as the Protestant Reformation.

In France, the Catholics chose to follow Rome and their pope. The king of France was called the "Most Christian King," and as king, Francois was bound to defend the Catholic Church. However, even he could see that there were problems within the church, and he felt sympathy for rising Protestants. In France, the Protestant reformers were called Huguenots. They followed the lead of John Calvin, who directed the movement from Geneva, Switzerland.

As the Huguenots' cause became more popular, Francois I puzzled over how to handle the growing push for reform. He wanted to support the Catholic Church, but Pope Clement VII had not yet turned over Catherine's full dowry. And the pope never would. In 1534, Clement VII died unexpectedly.

With the death of the pope, Catherine's political value sank to near zero. With the pope's territorial promises unfulfilled and Catherine's dowry only partly paid, a furious Francois claimed, "The girl has been given to me stark naked." Politically useless to her father-in-law and disliked by her husband, Catherine was miserable.

Henri de Valois' mistress, Diane de Poitiers (1499–1566)

It was obvious that Henri had no interest in his young wife. He preferred Diane de Poitiers, a noblewoman about 19 years older than he. Diane showed Henri concern, love, and attention—none of which the prince had received from his deceased mother, his unaffectionate father, or his disinterested stepmother.

Catherine compared herself

to Madame de Poitiers and found herself lacking. Diane was tall, slim, and blond while Catherine was short, dark, and dumpy. Diane was French, while Catherine was a foreigner. Catherine knew saying anything negative about Diane would not help her own situation, so she said nothing. Later in life, she said, "If I made good cheer for Madame [de Poitiers], it was [Henri] that I was really pleasing; for never did woman who loved her husband succeed in loving his [mistress]."

Diane de Poitiers and Catherine de Medici had more in common than an interest in Henri de Valois. Though Diane was French and Catherine Italian, they were actually second cousins through Catherine's mother. They shared a grandfather.

Her husband's mistress and the king's mistress were social enemies. They smiled on the surface, but they hated each other. Catherine walked a tightrope between the two women that was complicated somewhat by her entry into a group of women known as "La Petite Bande." This group was made up of accomplished and witty young ladies of court who rode with daring and told rude jokes. The king's mistress, Anne d'Hailly, Duchess d'Etampes, was the group's leader. She had to approve any new member of La Petite Bande. Luckily, the duchess admired Catherine's spirit and accepted her immediately.

But though she had made some friends and allies, Catherine's status at court was shaky, and after three years of marriage, it became even shakier. In 1536, the dauphin, Francois, played an energetic game of tennis with a gentleman from court. The prince became seriously overheated and asked for a cold glass of water. His secretary, an Italian count named Sebastian de Montecuculli, was sent for the water. After drinking, the prince immediately collapsed. He died eight days later.

The king was shocked. Suspicions arose that someone poisoned the young dauphin. A medical exam showed no poison and suggested nothing but a natural death. That was not acceptable to the king. Someone needed to be held responsible, and Sebastian de Montecuculli was the prime suspect. Montecuculli was questioned under severe torture. In agony and terror, he was pressured to make a confession. He was sentenced to "be drawn by four horses, and afterward the four parts of his body be hung at the four gates of the town of Lyons and his head put on the end of a lance which shall be place on the bridge over the Rhone [River]."

Modern medical opinion now holds that the dauphin probably died of pleurisy, a disease in which the lining of the lungs becomes dangerously inflamed.

Catherine's position at court was damaged by the death of her brother-in-law. People began to whisper about how Henri and Catherine, as the new dauphin and dauphine, were the only ones to really benefit from the death of Francois. Poison, which Montecuculli was said to have used, was at the time considered to be a particularly Italian method of murder, and no one in France had forgotten that Catherine was Italian. Furthermore, Montecuculli had come to France with a group of Italians accompanying Catherine. Rumors began to swirl around the new dauphine.

But Catherine had an even more serious problem than these rumors: She had still not borne a child. Since that was her main job, she risked being divorced for not producing an heir. Desperate, Catherine took advantage of all the modern medical wonders available to help a woman who had trouble getting pregnant. She was bled at the elbow and foot. She drank a cocktail made of mare's milk, rabbit's blood, and sheep urine. She rubbed medicines on her body made from cow dung and herbs. She even drank mule urine. Not surprisingly, none of these 16th-century medical miracles worked. It is surprising that she survived the treatments at all.

The status of women during Catherine's time fell somewhere below oxen and sheep. After all, oxen could pull carts, and sheep provided wool. A woman's sole value in life came from producing children. If no children arrived, that was considered the woman's fault. In Catherine's case, not being able to fulfill her role and provide the dauphin with children was not only a personal concern but one that threatened the claim to power of the entire royal family.

At the time, bloodletting was a common treatment for many different ailments.

Fearing she would be cast aside, Catherine went to Francois I and lay at his feet. She offered to give up her marriage and become a nun. Or, if possible, she'd remain in the court and serve Dauphin Henri's new wife. Francois, taken by her pleas, said:

My daughter, have no fear. Since God has willed that you should be my daughter-in-law and wife of the Dauphin, I do not wish to make any change, and perhaps it will please Almighty God to grant to you and to me the gift we so much long for.

At long last, Catherine became pregnant and gave birth to a boy in January 1544. Henri and Catherine named the boy Francois after his grandfather. She gave birth to a daughter, whom she named Elisabeth, the following year.

Dauphin Henri grew increasingly attached to his mistress, Diane. Catherine was powerless to do anything but produce more children and care for them. Even in that, she could not fault Diane. Madame de Poitiers loved the children dearly, treated them well, and showed great concern over their welfare.

In 1544, Francois I once again headed to war. This time, he was defending his honor against a slight by the Holy Roman Emperor Charles V. The war was quick and the peace treaty that followed promised a bride for Dauphin Henri's brother Charles. Charles would marry either the emperor's daughter or his niece, making Charles more powerful than the dauphin. Henri was furious. How could his father slight him so?

Henri need not have worried. Within a year, black plague swept over France. Foolhardy young Charles and his friends were out carousing when they came upon an empty cottage. Former tenants had died of the plague. Charles went in the house and tore up the contents. By nightfall, he had a fever. Within three days, he was dead.

The king's health had been declining for some

The bubonic plague ravaged Europe from the mid-1300s through the late 1600s.

time. He complained of bladder infections, sores that oozed pus, and other illnesses. While traveling in 1547, Francois I fell ill. He took shelter in Rambouillet. His doctors were called to provide a diagnosis: The king was rotting from the inside out. Whether it was cancer, infection, or another illness didn't matter. On March 31, 1547, King Francois I died. The king's heart and inner organs were removed and buried. His body was embalmed, and his followers offered the corpse food and wine for 11 days, as was the custom at the time.

When the funeral feasting ended, the burial service began. King Francois I was laid in a tomb in Saint-Denis. The cry went up, *"Le roi est mort! Vive le roi."* The old king was dead. Long live the new king, Henri II. ❧

Chapter

4 Queen of France

Catherine was 28 years old and still spoke with an Italian accent when she ascended the throne as queen of France. Her husband, Henri II, was crowned at Rheims on July 26, 1547. He was 28 as well, but he acted like a child. Henri had a strong and powerful body but a moody personality. He was slow to make decisions, but he rarely changed his mind once he decided to do something. A historian reflected, "His intelligence is not of the readiest, and yet it is such men as he who often succeed best."

Henri quickly got rid of all his father's closest advisers, including the Duchess d'Etampes. Henri's long-time friend, Anne Montmorency, had lost favor with the previous king. He was brought back to the court, however, and became one of Henri's

Although she became queen when Henri II was crowned in 1547, Catherine was not crowned herself until 1549.

> *To honor Diane, Henri designed an artistic initial that mingled his "H" with her "D." The work was so well done that one might have thought the initials were "H" and "C" for Catherine—but everyone knew it was not. Henri began wearing Diane's colors, black and white, at tournaments.*

most trusted advisers.

The new king's first acts included giving money and property to Diane de Poitiers. He also gave her the crown jewels, and a title: Duchess de Valentinois. Diane's position at court was that of friend, mistress, and adviser. The Spanish ambassador, St. Maurris, said of Diane's relationship to the king, "The worst is that the king lets himself be led and does everything that [Valentinois] and his lords advise, which drives the people to despair."

Catherine was now queen of France, but she remained second in the eyes of her husband. She was also pregnant again, and she delivered a second daughter, Claude, the year that Henri was crowned.

In 1549, Henri II decided to have Catherine crowned as queen. Catherine's joy was dampened by Diane's presence at the ceremony. As Duchess de Valentinois, Diane now walked among France's noble women at the crowning. Catherine knelt to accept the crown, but it was Diane standing by the king's side.

As king, Henri II defended the Catholic faith. His father had sympathized with the Protestant reformers, but Henri did not. His goal was to stop the growth of Protestantism, and he set up a special court to hear cases about heresy. The court, called the *chambre ardente* or burning room, issued dreadful sentences to the guilty. Laws became tighter and torture more horrible. Executions drew big audiences.

Crowds gathered in the public squares to watch punishments. People's bones cracked on the rack or the wheel. Their bodies burned at the stake. They were whipped, beaten, and killed. Yet, the Protestant

At King Henri's orders, French Protestants were hanged and burned simultaneously.

movement did not slow down. Under Henri's nose, the Huguenots built their first official church in Paris.

Catherine did not understand all the fuss about religion, and she disagreed with her husband's harsh treatment of the Protestant reformers. Although she had grown up Catholic and was related to several popes, she did not hold strong religious beliefs. She did not see the Huguenots as a threat. She even agreed with some of their reform ideas.

Perhaps it was the way Henri publicly embarrassed Catherine that made her sympathize with others who were treated poorly. Once, when Henri's court went to Lyons, Henri and Diane entered the city

King Henri II (1519–1559)

together. A great fanfare proclaimed their arrival. Groups of citizens acted out scenes honoring Diana, the goddess of the hunt, and banners in black and white, embroidered with the ornamental initials "H" and "D," fluttered in the breeze.

Custom declared that Queen Catherine enter the city the following day. Henri had Catherine's arrival delayed until evening. By the time she entered Lyons, the sun had set. Few people bothered to cheer the queen. Catherine was angry and ashamed.

Catherine returned to court to fulfill her main function in life: producing children. She gave birth to a son, Louis, in 1549, but the infant prince was sickly and died within a few months. The following year, Charles-Maximilien was born in June, followed by another son, Edouard-Alexandre, in 1551. So far, Catherine's children were a sickly lot. They had weak lungs and were prone to coughs, colds, and tuberculosis.

In 1552, Henri II decided to go to war against Charles V, the Holy Roman Emperor. Henri blamed Charles for the years he had spent imprisoned in Spain. The king never forgave his father for those years, and he didn't excuse Charles' part either.

Finally, Henri acknowledged Catherine. He appointed her regent. She was finally able to take on a task that supported both her husband and her adopted country. To her annoyance, she shared her role with Jean Bertrand, the Keeper of the Seals and a staunch supporter of Diane de Poitiers. Catherine

Many kingdoms used regents when their king or queen was unable to rule. Sometimes, a king went to war, leaving a regent in charge. That regent could be his wife, another relative, or a political leader. When a ruler died and his or her heir was too young to rule, a regent took over until the monarch reached adulthood.

couldn't make any decisions and had to consult the king's council on everything.

Catherine dedicated herself to living up to her husband's trust. She gathered and arranged shipping of supplies and weapons. She made sure the army had enough food to eat and bullets to shoot. And, she arranged for the money needed to support the war effort. She proved herself to be intelligent and capable in her role as regent.

Henri's first venture as a military leader proved a great success as well. He took possession of Lorraine with little cost in lives or money. In response, Emperor Charles' army lay siege to the French city of Metz. For 45 days, the emperor's army bombarded Metz. No food or supplies entered the city gates.

Fortunately, the French troops had Francois, Duke of Guise, for their leader. Stuck in Metz, Guise rallied his 6,000 troops to defend the city against Charles' army. They broke the siege. Cold, hungry, and without pay, Charles' soldiers finally gave up. Guise became an instant hero.

But war has always been expensive, and Henri spent far too much money defending his honor. Besides, he became bored with war. He longed to return home to Diane. And of course his wife and children were there, too.

In 1553, Catherine gave birth to Marguerite, her only truly healthy child. This daughter, called Margot,

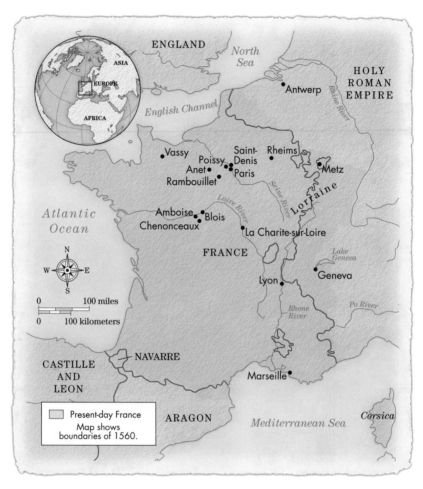

The France of Catherine's time looked much as it does today.

beamed good health, which her mother resented. Why were her sons so sickly while this girl was so healthy? Since she knew Margot and her other daughters would marry out of the family, Catherine showed less interest in them than she did for her sons. Her pet was Edouard-Alexandre; her least favorite was Margot.

Francois-Hercules was the last son born to Henri and Catherine. Early in his life, he contracted

Queen Catherine and King Henri had a large family of seven children.

smallpox, which left his skin deeply pocked and ugly. His spine was twisted, forming a hunchback. It was a cruel joke that he was named Hercules. As a boy, Francois-Hercules reportedly entertained himself torturing animals, roasting rabbits alive, and killing birds.

By 1556, Catherine had given birth to eight children, seven of whom had survived. Now, she was pregnant again, this time with twin girls whom she named Jeanne and Victoire. Jeanne died during the birth, and Victoire survived only a few weeks. Catherine herself nearly died during the delivery. There would be no more children for the Valois king and queen.

Henri II busied himself with stemming the growth of Protestantism. In 1557, he issued the Edict of Compiegne, a document in which he declared war on heretics. Within weeks, more than 130 people were arrested for following the teachings of John Calvin. Their religion, now called the Huguenot faith, was banned within France's cities and towns. Many Protestants stood trial for their beliefs, and three were executed for heresy.

As the Valois children moved into their teens, it came time for them to marry. Catherine helped engineer marriages that would increase her family's power within Europe and help maintain their rule. Catherine's oldest son, Dauphin Francois, was to

Until quite recently, childbirth was an exceedingly risky business, and many women died during the process. Delivery often caused severe bleeding, blood poisoning, and other complications from which mothers frequently died. Those who survived delivery often were prescribed treatments that made them weaker, not stronger. The fact that Catherine was able to successfully deliver so many children is testament to her strong spirit and sturdy constitution.

marry young Mary Stuart, Queen of Scots, as part of a political plan to ally Scotland and France. Mary was the daughter of King James of Scotland and Marie de Guise, a member of France's influential Guise family and relative of Francois, Duke of Guise. She was also heir to the English throne through her grandmother, Margaret Tudor. When she was only 6 days old, her father died, and Mary became a queen—and a political pawn.

Mary Stuart became queen of Scotland when she was only an infant.

Mary had moved to the French court as a child, and she and Francois became close friends. Their marriage, which had been planned since childhood,

finally took place on April 24, 1558. Francois was 14, and Mary was 15. To honor Mary's position as queen of Scotland, she was called the "queen dauphine," and Francois, who was now also king of Scotland, was the "king dauphin."

More Valois marriages took place the following year. In January 1559, Princess Claude married Charles III, Duke of Lorraine. This allied the powerful, independent region of Lorraine to France. The next wedding took place on June 22 between Elisabeth and Spain's King Felipe II. Felipe did not attend the wedding. Instead, he sent a stand-in. Elisabeth would meet her bridegroom later. The third wedding was planned for July. It would unite the king's sister, Marguerite, to Emmanuel-Philibert of Savoy.

Between the final two weddings, Henri held a tournament. Henri, an able jouster, issued a challenge to all comers. Catherine felt uneasy. A seer named Nostradamus had published a prophecy that read:

> *The young lion will overcome the old,*
> *in a field of combat in a single fight.*
> *He will pierce his eyes in a golden cage,*
> *two wounds in one, he then dies a*
> *cruel death.*

Catherine felt certain the prophecy warned of Henri's death. On June 30, 1559, King Henri II entered the tournament. After defeating the first challengers,

Though her reliance on astrologers contributed to Catherine's sinister reputation over the years, reliance on the prophecies of seers such as Nostradamus was typical of the time. Everyone who could afford it consulted with astrologers. Catherine was believed to have prophetic abilities as well, and she accurately predicted the deaths of loved ones based on her dreams.

he faced a young knight named Montgomery. The knight got the better of the king, who insisted on a second chance.

The horses thundered down the lists. Two passes led to two misses, but the third pass proved a disaster. Montgomery's lance struck Henri II and shattered. A 4-inch-long (10-centimeter-long) splinter slipped under the king's helmet and into his eye. Blood poured from the wound. The king fainted from the pain.

The surgeons didn't know what to do. They removed as much of the splinter as they could but could not heal the wound. They packed the wound with herbs and egg white. Doctors experimented on the skulls of four criminals who had been beheaded, but they found no cure. Catherine wept by her husband's side. For days, the king lay in agony. Infection set in, and the wound simply continued to fester.

On July 8, the king rallied and insisted that his sister's wedding take place. But instead of an elegant church ceremony, Marguerite got a quick Mass the following evening in Elisabeth's room. Catherine refused to leave her husband to attend the wedding.

In the palace, Diane de Poitiers waited anxiously.

She could not go to Henri because Catherine was there, but she prayed for the king to survive. She said, "As long as there is a single breath of life in him … I am still invincible." But Henri did not have many breaths left. He died on July 10, 1559.

Fulfilling Nostradamus' prophecy, King Henri was fatally injured while jousting in a tournament.

Dauphin Francois—just 15 years old—was now king. What could he know about ruling a country? And so, with the death of her husband, Queen Catherine became the queen mother and an increasingly powerful force in French rule. ❧

Chapter

5 THE QUEEN MOTHER

⟨๑ᢓᢓᢓᢓ⟩

Catherine was in deep mourning. Despite the many times Henri II had shamed her, she had loved him deeply. She kept her rooms dark to match her overwhelming sorrow. One of Catherine's friends recalled:

> She was in a room entirely hung with black sheets so that not only the walls and windows, but the floor as well was covered with them. There were no lights save two candles burning on a small altar which was also covered in black.

In her new role as the queen mother, Catherine wore black gowns and veils. Her voice trembled as she spoke. Visitors leaned close to hear her because her voice barely rose above a whisper. Mourning

After the death of her husband, Catherine wore mourning attire for the rest of her life.

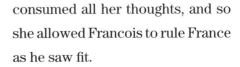

One of Francois' first orders as king was to take back some of the gifts his father had given Diane de Poitiers, including the crown jewels. Catherine demanded that she give her the estate at Chenonceaux. Diane retreated to her estate at Anet.

consumed all her thoughts, and so she allowed Francois to rule France as he saw fit.

French law allowed a king 14 years old or more to rule, and at the time he became king, Francois was old enough by one year. However, he had no training, interest, or ability for ruling. What's more, he was prone to high fevers and lung disease. The young king needed help, and he looked to his wife's uncles, the Duke of Guise and the Cardinal of Lorraine, for guidance. They would manage France's dealings with other countries, as well as oversee the kingdom's army and finances.

France had serious money trouble. Henri II had been a big spender. He borrowed money for wars, lived extravagantly, and lavished gifts on Diane de Poitiers. He promised huge dowries for Elisabeth and Marguerite, both of which went unpaid. The king's debts added up to 40 million *livres*, but the royal income was only 12 million livres. The French throne was going bankrupt.

The Duke of Guise tried to bring spending in line with the income. He cut government salaries and told the people owed money to live without it. Expenses were cut back so drastically that even the king's crowning ceremony was a low-budget event.

While the Duke of Guise attended to the money, the Cardinal of Lorraine addressed the issue of France's religion. Like Henri II before him, the Cardinal of Lorraine felt duty-bound to wipe out Protestantism. He focused on Anne du Bourg,

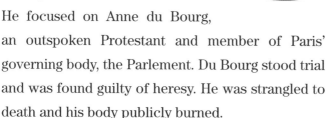

Francois de Lorraine, Duke of Guise (1510–1563)

an outspoken Protestant and member of Paris' governing body, the Parlement. Du Bourg stood trial and was found guilty of heresy. He was strangled to death and his body publicly burned.

But Catherine was not very religious herself and didn't understand the religious fervor that surrounded her. In fact, she felt sympathy for the Protestant cause. She said:

> *When I see these poor folk burnt, bruised and tormented, not for thieving and marauding but simply for upholding their own opinions; when I see some of them suffer cheerfully, with a glad heart, I am*

moved to believe that there is something in this which [passes] human reason.

So, while the cardinal roasted heretics at the stake, Catherine went into action. She asked the government to pass the Edict of Toleration, a law intended to stop the abuse of Protestants. While the law allowed Protestants to worship freely, it did not change the minds of Catholics about the dangers of Protestantism. French Catholics continued to burn with fury over the Huguenots and their cause.

Within the year, Francois II took to his sickbed with a high fever and painful headaches. An ear infection oozed pus, and Queen Mary and Catherine sat by Francois' bedside. The infection lingered, keeping the king in agony. Finally, on December 5, 1560, King Francois II died.

With Francois' death, Catherine's second son, 10-year-old Charles-Maximilien, succeeded his brother as the new king. But Catherine had no intention of stepping out of the picture this time. She declared:

Since it has pleased God to deprive me of my elder son, I mean to submit to the Divine will and to assist and serve the King, my second son, in the feeble measure of my experience. ... I have decided to keep him beside me, and to rule the State as a devoted mother must do.

Catherine became the regent of France since her son, now Charles IX, was still too young to rule. She was again at the helm of French affairs. ❧

With the death of her son Francois II, Catherine became the most powerful person in France.

6 WARS OF RELIGION

Without a strong king to lead the country, France began to fall apart. Running the government became a wrestling match between the Catholics and the Huguenots. Both groups wanted power. Each side had armed camps waiting for battle. Each had spies checking out the actions of their enemies.

In 1561, an advisory group called the Estates-General met to discuss France's increasing financial difficulties. The country needed money, and the peasants and merchants could not pay any more taxes. The Catholic Church, however, was incredibly rich, and it had never paid taxes. In a rare instance in history, the nobles and general population banded together against the church. Selling off church property might produce 120 million livres and pay off

French Protestants, or Huguenots, were brutally persecuted by Catholics in France.

France formed a group of representatives to provide advice for the government called the Estates-General. The group consisted of Catholic leaders, the nobility, and other citizens. Each section had one vote. Although this might seem fair, the "other citizens" group equaled 95 percent of the population. Other than advice and taxes, the Estates-General had no real power. It was not a representative body like Congress. Final word came from the king or the regent. Thus, Catherine, as regent, held power over the entire kingdom.

the royal debt. It was, they said, the church's turn to pay.

The clergy moved to the French city of Poissy for a conference. They were joined by the royal family, the king's council, and representatives of the Huguenots. The Huguenots voiced their thoughts and beliefs. The Catholic clergy replied the same way they had for years. The Catholic Church changed at a snail's pace. Nothing was—or would be—resolved.

The Catholics worried that the Huguenots had too much influence over the royal family. It was reported that the royal children said their prayers in French instead of Latin—a Huguenot practice. In response, the Catholics decided to kidnap the king's brother, Edouard-Alexandre. With the young dauphin in their keeping, the Catholics could force the king to act against the Protestants. Their plot backfired.

Edouard-Alexandre learned of the plot when the Catholic group suggested he come willingly. He, in turn, told his mother about the planned kidnapping.

Catherine was furious. She said, "I was so astonished that I could hardly believe it." Catherine increased the palace guards and ordered windows walled up. The Catholics claimed the plot was just a joke, but Catherine, always protective of her children, didn't believe them. The Catholics lost ground with Catherine, who continued to sympathize with the Huguenots.

Catherine had hoped that the conference in Poissy would help the Catholics and Protestants resolve their differences.

Meanwhile, Catholics and Protestants clashed throughout the country. Huguenots destroyed churches, broke stained glass windows, and damaged religious art. Riots broke out in Paris, leaving many Protestants and Catholics injured.

Once again, Catherine attempted to find a middle ground for the two groups. In 1562, she forced through the Edict of January. This document allowed Protestants to hold religious services in France as long as they were outside town or city walls. Catherine hoped that this act would bring peace to the kingdom. But then came Vassy.

In March, while visiting family, the Duke of Guise stopped in Vassy, a small walled city. He heard Huguenots singing hymns in a barn that stood within the city walls—illegal under the new law. Guise attended a nearby Catholic Mass, and he still heard the Huguenots while he prayed. Enraged, he sent his armed men to the barn to deal with the Huguenots. In the resulting fight, 23 Huguenots were confirmed killed, although later sources swelled the number to 74. More than 100 were injured. Guise and his men suffered only minor scrapes and scratches. This incident, known as the "Massacre at Vassy," was to have far-reaching effects. Guise's actions served to validate violence against Protestants and sparked the series of engagements known as the French Wars of Religion.

Catherine recognized the direction in which things were heading, and she appealed to Louis de Conde, the primary Huguenot leader, to react with reason and to help find a remedy for the violence. She wrote:

If it were not for the trust which I place in God and in the assurance of your help to keep this kingdom and to serve the king my son, I would feel even worse. … I hope that we shall be able to find a remedy for every-thing with your good advice and help.

The Massacre at Vassy was the beginning of the French Wars of Religion.

But neither side, Protestant nor Catholic, was willing to give an inch. Condé and his relative Admiral Gaspard de Coligny assembled a Huguenot army, and Guise and Lorraine formed a Catholic army. Both sides claimed to stand staunchly behind the king.

The first War of Religion had begun.

Catherine tried to negotiate a truce, but neither side trusted her. The Huguenots had done as she asked and removed themselves from Paris, only to be branded as traitors and enemies of France. The Catholics thought Catherine too close to the Huguenots. Catherine, thoroughly discouraged, could only say, "I am very upset that it will be said throughout Christendom that it is I—although I have been so concerned about the honor of this country—

During the Wars of Religion, many Huguenots left the city of Paris, and the country of France as well.

who am responsible for ruining it."

In the midst of the fighting, the Duke of Guise was assassinated, shot in the back by a young man named Poltrot de Mere. At first, Mere claimed that Admiral Coligny had hired him, but he soon changed his story to claim that Coligny knew nothing about the assassination. The Huguenots swore Coligny was a man of honor and would never be responsible for shooting a man in the back. But it didn't matter what Mere and the Huguenots said. The Catholics were positive that the Huguenots and Coligny were responsible for the Duke of Guise's death.

Privately, Catherine may have found the death of Guise convenient. She was glad she would no longer have to manage his fanaticism. Publicly, however, she mourned the death of France's hero. She delivered a speech at the duke's funeral:

> *By the most miserable of deaths [God] has taken from me the one man who stood out alone and devoted himself to the King. M de Guise was the greatest captain in our realm and one of the greatest and worthiest ministers the King could ever be served by.*

Whether Admiral Coligny was involved in the assassination or not, Catherine was certain that he, once a close friend and adviser, would fall and bring

From a noble family, Admiral Gaspard de Coligny (1519–1572) served as a colonel in the French infantry, as well as a naval admiral. He was also a Protestant leader and would later become King Charles IX's favorite adviser. In his youth, Coligny founded two unsuccessful colonies in the New World.

the king down with him. She wrote to her sister-in-law, Marguerite of Savoy, about Coligny, calling him

this man of good, who says nothing but for religion, but tries to have us all killed. I fear that during this war, he will eventually kill my children and get rid of my best men.

As Catherine's son Charles IX approached his teens, she decided it was time to declare him old enough to rule. Charles was a weak, sickly, scrawny teenager with an ugly birthmark on his face. Behind his back, people called him the "snotty king" or the "brat king"—and no wonder: Charles had some serious mental problems. He joined hunts with a frenzy that worried the rest of the party and often threw temper tantrums that would have embarrassed a 2-year-old. Still, it was time for Catherine and her advisers to begin teaching him how to rule. Catherine would step down as regent, and Charles would be the king.

The queen mother planned a progress to introduce the king to his kingdom, similar to the tours taken by Francois I when Catherine was newly married. She

hoped the tour, which would take a couple of years, would help diffuse the civil war.

In 1564, Charles IX's traveling court embarked on their royal progress. It included the master of household, 100 gentlemen, a Swiss guard, and a Scottish guard. Grooms attended the horses, and

Catherine ruled France as regent for Charles IX for four years.

King Charles IX (1550–1574)

maids and valets attended ladies and gentlemen. The royals needed doctors and druggists to heal them, cooks and bakers to feed them, musicians to entertain them, and barbers to shave them. Along with this massive group went beds and bedding, pots and pans, spices, utensils, chairs, tables, and even paintings and tapestries. All this required enough servants to populate a medium-sized city. Great in size, the progress progressed very slowly. It easily took a week to shift the group from one town to the next—a mere 20 miles (32 kilometers) away.

The high point of the tour was to be a meeting with Catherine's daughter, Elisabeth. In 1565, the family met along the border between France and Spain. Catherine commented that her daughter had become very Spanish in her clothes, speech, and general attitude. This was only natural, since Elisabeth was Spain's queen. Elisabeth, speaking on behalf of her husband the king, urged her mother to stamp out Protestantism in France. Catherine had to

Catherine's eldest daughter, Queen Elisabeth of Spain (1545–1568)

refuse. There was no clear solution to the Huguenot problem, and she was eager to avoid more civil war.

Yet more civil war did follow. Over the next 36 years, France was consumed by six religious wars and a number of smaller encounters. Churches lay in ruins and fields lay empty, as both armies marched over crops and took cattle for food. Worse, the battles pitted brother against brother, father against son, and neighbor against neighbor. Anger and hatred took on a life of its own. And through it all, Catherine tried to find a middle ground, unable to understand the depths of the religious passion around her, unsure how to heal her adopted country. ॐ

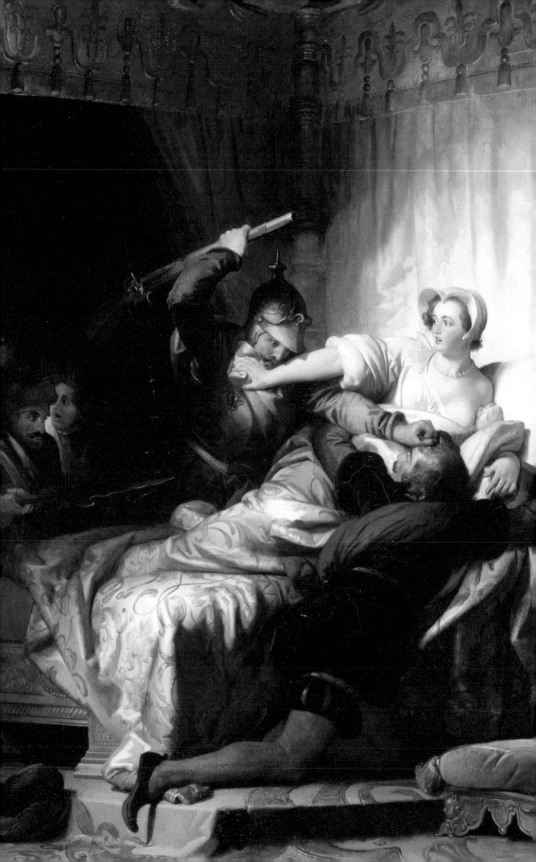

7 MURDER AND MAYHEM

❧❧❧

France was in trouble. Religious differences continued to carve the kingdom into pieces. On one side stood the stern, grim-faced Huguenots, now led by Admiral Gaspard de Coligny. Their Protestant religion spread and their political power grew. On the other side stood the Roman Catholic Church, along with centuries of French history. In the middle stood King Charles IX and the queen mother. The Valois family was the rope in the tug-of-war pulling France apart.

Meanwhile, violence gripped the kingdom's cities and towns. Murders became everyday events. Every time peace seemed possible, another assassination took place. The continual violence made people edgy, and the strain led to even more violence.

On St. Bartholomew's Day, 1572, French Huguenots were attacked and killed throughout Paris—even in the royal apartment of Margot, Queen of Navarre.

King Charles IX hired 6,000 Swiss guards to boost up his army. The Huguenots, in turn, hired help from Protestant mercenaries in Germany. Then, in 1567, the Huguenots made a daring strike. They moved close to Paris and blockaded the city's roads and waterways. No food or goods entered Paris, and its citizens grew hungry—and angry. The Huguenots and the royal army battled on a field near Paris. In that battle, the royal family's old friend, Montmorency, died. When King Charles wanted to sue for peace, Paris' citizens countered by offering money to support the war. They didn't want peace with the Huguenots. Catherine feared that a true peace would never be reached.

While religious wars consumed the country, Catherine attended to the business of being a mother.

A 16th-century engraving depicts two paths of religion: Catholicism and Protestantism.

She continued to educate Charles in kingship and grieved the loss of her daughter Elisabeth, who died in childbirth in 1568.

The year 1570 brought Catherine and her family a respite from grieving and thoughts of war. Catherine had engineered a union between her son King Charles and Elizabeth of Austria, daughter of the Holy Roman Emperor. This marriage would ally France with the massive and powerful Holy Roman Empire.

But Catherine's power-brokering did not end with Charles' wedding. She offered her son Edouard-Alexandre, now the Duke of Anjou, as a match to Queen Elizabeth I of England. The fact that he was 19 years old to Elizabeth's 37 did not bother Catherine. She was power building.

The Duke of Anjou was tall, slim, and well-built. His face was handsome but marred by a gaping, oozing hole, called a fistula, between his right eye and his nose. Like most of Catherine's children, he suffered from weak lungs.

The duke refused the match, so Catherine switched her offer to her youngest son, Francois-Hercules. At 15, Francois-Hercules was short, hunchbacked, stunted, and the ugliest member of the Valois family. His most noticeable feature was a large, bulging nose that dominated his face. Surprisingly, Queen Elizabeth I did not laugh at the offer. She toyed with the idea for several months, but in the end, the queen declined to marry Francois-Hercules.

Catherine's matchmaking skills had failed with her two sons, but there was still a daughter. She had originally hoped to wed Margot, her youngest daughter, to Don Carlos, the Spanish king's son. That would link Spain and France doubly, through the marriages of Elisabeth to Felipe II, King of Spain, and Margot to Felipe's son. She hoped the match would help the Valois family remain dominant in European rule.

Unfortunately, Don Carlos was dangerously insane. King Felipe put his son in prison for his own safety, as well as for the safety of others. Instead, Catherine took another approach and decided to try to patch the rift between the Catholics and Huguenots by marrying Margot to Henri, the King of Navarre and a Huguenot leader. Like her brothers, Margot was less than thrilled about the match her mother offered. She would have refused outright, but young women didn't have the same rights as their brothers.

The wedding festivities were scheduled to begin with the

The kingdom of Navarre lay on the slopes of the Pyrenees, between France and Spain. In the early 1500s, the southern part of Navarre became part of Spain. The northern section remained a separate kingdom with Bearn as its capital. The last king of Navarre was Henri III, Catherine's son-in-law. When King Henri III of France died in 1589, Henri of Navarre succeeded to the French throne as Henri IV. Navarre officially became part of France under Louis XIII, Henri IV's son.

wedding ceremony on August 18, 1572, and were to run for a full week. The ceremony itself went off smoothly, but what happened next was a disaster. Huguenots had flocked to Paris, expecting the union to bring more religious tolerance to the city. After all, how could King Charles reject Protestantism when his own sister was married to a Huguenot leader?

But Catherine had unfinished plans. Earlier, she

Catherine and the king watched couples dance at the wedding festivities of Princess Margot and King Henri of Navarre.

had arranged the assassination of the Huguenot Coligny, an event that failed. To finish the task, plans were made to slay him and other Huguenot leaders on August 24—St. Bartholomew's Day.

King Charles himself took aim during the St. Bartholomew's Day Massacre.

Admiral Coligny had already survived one assassination attempt, and he was not surprised by the second attack. When the king's guard arrived at his townhouse to murder him, he ordered his men to leave. Coligny said, "For a long time now I have been preparing for death, save yourselves, for you cannot save me. I will commend my soul to God's mercy." He showed no fear as a guard pierced his chest with a sword.

Back at the king's palace, the Louvre, newly married Margot found herself in a trap. Her brother's Swiss guards swept the halls for Huguenots. Though a Huguenot leader, her new husband was safe because he was related to the king. Others were not so lucky. One Huguenot member of Henri's court pounded on Margot's door. When she opened it, he entered. Margot later wrote:

> [He was] wounded in the elbow by a sword and by a halberd on the arm, and [he] was pursued by four archers

In the 1500s, the Louvre was the French king's palace and stronghold in the heart of Paris. King Francois I got rid of the Louvre's palace library and began collecting art. He began his collection with 12 paintings by Titian, Raphael, and Leonardo da Vinci. By 1715, the Louvre housed 2,500 paintings, sculptures, and other art objects. The collection belonged to the king and was seen only by his guests. In 1793, however, the Louvre became a public museum. Today, it houses 300,000 works of art, although comparatively few are displayed. One of the Louvre's most valuable and popular paintings dates from Francois I's original collection— the Mona Lisa.

who followed him into the room. ... I had him laid in my closet and his wounds tended and kept him there until he recovered. ... Monsieur de Nançay told me what was happening and assured me that the King my husband was in the King's room and that no harm would come to him.

The attacks soon turned into an all-out massacre. Rumors spread that the king had authorized killing Protestants. That was all that most Catholics needed. All Paris lay gripped by a frenzy of murder and

mayhem, and the violence spread to other towns and cities as well. Sadly, the fate of Coligny's corpse paints an all-too-accurate picture of the mob's state of mind. The crowd cut pieces from the body as it was dragged through the streets. The corpse was then tossed into the Seine River. Later, someone pulled the body out of the water and hung it by the feet in a public square. The head, lopped off and embalmed, was packaged and sent to Pope Gregory XIII as a present.

Neither the king nor his mother could bring the situation under control. When the last of the dead had been buried and the last injuries tended, the death toll numbered in the thousands. Paris alone saw more than 2,000 dead.

Though she didn't order the massacre, the blame fell on Catherine. France's ambassador to Venice, Italy, explained what other Europeans thought:

> *Madame ... the massacres which have occurred throughout the whole kingdom of France, not only against the Admiral and other principal leaders of the religion, but against so many poor and innocent people, have so profoundly moved and altered the feeling of those here who are friendly to your Crown, even though all are Catholics, that they cannot be satisfied with any excuses, [blaming] everything that has been done to you alone and Monsieur d'Anjou.*

Catherine's reputation was damaged by the massacre, and she lost favor with European leaders. Still, there was hope for the Valois family. While murder and mayhem ran through Paris, an odd thing happened in Poland. The Polish king, Sigismund-Augustus, died without an heir. Poland went shopping for a new king and settled on Catherine's favorite son, the young Duke of Anjou. Catherine knew that her son would make an excellent king, but of course she had always been blind to his faults.

King Charles IX was not pleased to learn that his brother had been chosen to be king of Poland.

The duke wasn't quite as delighted with his future kingdom as his mother was, however. He had his eye on his brother's throne. He dawdled as long as he could, finally setting off for Poland in 1573. The

parting of the three brothers—the King of France, the soon-to-be King of Poland, and Francois-Hercules—who had become the Duke of Alencon—was strained at best. They each envied one another's situation, which did not make for brotherly love.

No sooner had the Duke of Anjou left for Poland when Charles IX fell ill. The king was in the final stages of tuberculosis. Fevers and headaches tormented him. He suffered sweats and shivering, and he vomited blood. By May 1574, Charles' body was little more than skin and bones. He returned to his bed. He made Catherine regent until Henri could return from Poland to assume the throne. Catherine and Charles' wife, Elizabeth, sat by his bed, waiting for the final breaths to rattle in his chest. On May 30, 1574, King Charles IX died.

Catherine immediately sent word to Poland for her son to return. However, the Poles had invested time and money in their new king and were not keen to give him up. He and his party sneaked out of Poland in the dead of night. The Poles chased after him. Perhaps they were trying to prevent him from leaving—or perhaps they wanted the Polish crown jewels he stuffed in his pockets before leaving. He may have been king, but he was also a thief. ❧

8 THE END OF THE VALOIS

❧

Catherine was delighted. Her favorite child had returned and sat on the French throne. He was crowned on February 13, 1575 and took the name Henri III. As king, one of his first tasks was to produce an heir, and that meant getting a wife. The Holy Roman Emperor hoped that Henri would marry Elizabeth, his brother's widow, but Henri had ideas of his own. He settled on Louise de Vaudemont, a relative of the powerful families of Guise and Lorraine. The pair married two days after Henri was crowned king.

At the time of her son's coronation and marriage, Catherine was 55 years old, and her extensive family had dwindled to three children. She had lost Louis, Jeanne, and Victoire as infants. Francois II and Charles IX had both died while king. Elisabeth, Queen of Spain, had died in childbirth, and Catherine's daughter Claude, Duchess of Lorraine, died in 1575. This left Henri III, the present king, Margot, Queen of Navarre, and Francois-Hercules, Duke of Alencon.

Henri III was not the robust, manly king France hoped for. He could waste hours on achieving the perfect hairdo. He took great care in choosing his clothes and even took to wearing a corset to give his body the perfect figure. Critics claimed he even dressed as a woman.

The fistula on his face, like a gaping wound, was a constant reminder of his poor health. An infected and oozing sore under his arm was a worry as well. And like the rest of Catherine's children, he was also prone to tuberculosis, the dreaded lung disease that had taken his brother Charles.

Henri was involved in the political life of France, but he was no leader. As a result, the court became a hotbed of plots and counterplots, a place of rumors and gossip. Henri of Navarre described his brother-in-law's court as "the strangest place on earth. We are nearly always ready to cut each other's throats. We carry daggers, wear coats of mail and often [an armored breastplate] beneath a cape."

Not surprisingly, years of religious wars had destroyed the country, and France was in ruins. King Henri didn't seem to notice. One observer wrote:

Everywhere one sees ruin, the livestock for the most part destroyed ... stretches of good land [unplanted] and many peasants forced to leave their homes and to become vagabonds ... The clergy and the nobility ... are also in hard circumstances, but particularly the nobility, who are completely ruined and indebted.

Catherine (at left) continued to wear black in mourning, even at her son Henri III's court ball.

But for all the trouble in the country, there was plenty at court as well. The Duke of Alencon had become involved in the Huguenot cause and pushed to gain more power in France. With the country, the court, and her family falling apart in front of her, Catherine begged the king to seek peace, no matter the cost. So on May 6, 1576, King Henri III signed the

Peace of Monsieur, a document that placed Protestantism on equal footing with Catholicism in France. Widows and orphans from the St. Bartholomew's Day Massacre would receive pensions. And the Protestants took control of eight major cities in France. Henri wept as he signed his name, blaming his bossy mother and his revolting brother for putting him in such an embarrassing situation.

Despite the Peace of Monsieur, France was not ready for peace. War broke out again in the south, and Henri sent the royal army to capture the Protestant city of La Charite-sur-Loire.

Wars cost plenty, however, and the king had run out of money. Henri decided it was time for a permanent peace. In 1578, Henri signed yet another treaty, and Catherine headed off to the war-torn regions on a peace mission. The Protestants may not have liked her much, but they had to respect her. She rode into Protestant strongholds with her head held high. She appeared open and pleasant at all times with no snobbishness.

Meanwhile, Francois-Hercules, who became Duke of Anjou as part of the Peace of Monsieur, went to England to pursue Queen Elizabeth, but he was rejected again. After returning to France, he headed for Antwerp to lead a battle against the Spaniards. Many French nobles died in the fighting, and the duke found himself accused of being a criminal. Alencon's disappointment with Queen Elizabeth and his defeat at Antwerp affected his already poor health. Like Charles before him, he fell ill with fevers and chills, and he vomited blood. He died of tuberculosis on June 10, 1584.

With Alencon now dead, the Valois family had no heir to the throne. Catherine was desperate to keep the crown in the family, and she prayed that Henri and Louise would have a child. Her prayers were in vain. Henri III could produce no heir for France.

Everyone wanted a say in deciding who could be the next king. King Henri III wanted the King of Navarre to take over, but the pope cut the kingdom of Navarre off from the church and said that Protestant princes could not rule France.

Once again, France went to war. This war, called the War of the Three Henris, was fought among the different groups with an interest in the French throne. The first Henri was Henri III, the present king of France. His brother-in-law, King Henri of Navarre, was a Huguenot leader and the Protestants' choice to rule. And finally, Henri de Guise, who became the Duke of Guise after the assassination of his father, Francois, was a Catholic leader and the Catholics' hope for king.

By this time, Catherine was already approaching 70, an ancient age for people in the 1500s. She had all the aches, pains, and problems of an old woman. Added to all that, she had weak lungs and the stress of troublesome children. Her son the king seemed to be losing his mind. He became a devout Catholic. He went on long pilgrimages by foot and whipped himself as punishment for his sins. The young king also took a morbid interest in death. He had skulls embroidered on his clothes and decorated a room with skeleton parts stolen from a cemetery.

Catherine's other children and relations gave her cause for worry as well. Margot ran away from her husband and went to live with the Duke of Lorraine, her brother-in-law. And Mary, Queen of Scots—Catherine's first

Henri III
(1551–1589)

daughter-in-law—was forced out of Scotland. Queen Elizabeth of England saw Mary as a threat and had her beheaded.

Meanwhile, the War of the Three Henris wore on. Catherine continued to advise her son, as she had done throughout his reign, but King Henri shrugged off his mother's advice. He would be his own man and make his own decisions. Unfortunately, one of these decisions was a grave mistake. Henri de Guise had refused the king any support unless the king excluded Navarre from succession to the French throne. Henri III decided to kill Guise. He ordered the major members of the Guise family brought to Blois, where the Estates-General was meeting. The king's guards fell on the Duke of Guise and stabbed him to death. Guise's brother, a cardinal in the church, suffered a similar fate. Then, Henri III had the bodies burned.

Henri called on his mother, who was sick in bed. He said, "Good day, Madam. Please forgive me. M de Guise is dead. … I have had him killed." Catherine was shocked. She saw disaster ahead but could do nothing. She said of her son, "I see him rushing towards his ruin. I am afraid he may lose his body, soul, and kingdom." Henri fled Paris to avoid the revenge of Guise's followers.

Catherine's prediction was right, but she didn't live to see Henri's fall. She never left her bed again.

Sixty-nine-year-old Catherine de Medici de Valois died a few days later, on January 5, 1589. It was a fitting date for the death of a onetime queen and mother to three kings, because that day is known in France as *Le Jour des Rois*, or the "Day of Kings."

Although she should have been buried in Saint-Denis along with her husband, France was in turmoil. Because of the unrest following Henri's assassination of Guise, there was fear that Catherine's body might be dragged through the streets if it remained in Paris. Her body was secretly buried, under cover of darkness, in an unmarked grave in Saint-Sauveur churchyard in Blois. Later, she would be buried a second time in the Valois family chapel at Saint-Denis.

With the end of Catherine, the dynasty she had worked so hard to preseve neared its end as well. After his mother's death, Henri III stayed with his troops on the outskirts of Paris. One night at the camp, a young clergyman named Jacques Clement came with papers addressed to Henri. Clement, claiming to have a secret message, leaned closer to whisper in the king's ear. As he did so, he stabbed Henri III in the stomach. The king died of his wounds the following morning.

Henri's death ended the reign of the Valois family. Henri of Navarre became King Henri IV, the first Protestant king of France. All that Catherine had fought to hold ended with a whisper and a sharp dagger.

History has painted Catherine de Medici both as a scheming villain and a victim of circumstance, but in truth she was neither. Her role and her contributions were much more complex. She was an orphan, princess, queen, regent, and mother. She was also a woman working within a male power structure. She was a foreign-born commoner who rose to rule an adopted country. She was a practical person in an age marked by fanaticism. And, as she worked behind the scenes to make peace between the warring Catholics and Protestants and to preserve her family's rule, she became more influential than any of the kings in her life. She was the true power behind the French throne. ஓ

Catherine de Medici (1519–1589)

DE MEDICI'S LIFE

1519
Born on April 13 in
Florence, Italy

1527
Enters convent
school

1533
Marries Henri de
Valois, second-in-line
to the French throne

1520

1524
German peasants rise
up against their land-
lords in the Peasant's
War, the greatest
mass uprising in
German history

1531
The "great comet,"
later called Halley's
Comet, causes a wave
of superstition

WORLD EVENTS

1544

Gives birth to first child, a son named Francois

1536

Becomes dauphine of France when Henri's brother Francois dies

1547

Becomes queen of France with death of Francois I

1535

The first complete English translation of the Bible is printed in Germany

1545

The Catholic Counter-Reformation begins in Europe

DE MEDICI'S LIFE

1552

Is temporarily appointed regent when Henri II goes to war against the Holy Roman Empire

1556

Gives birth to last children, twins Jeanne and Victoire, both of whom die as infants

1559

Becomes queen mother and goes into mourning when Henri II dies and son Francois II becomes king

1550

1555

Artist Michelangelo completes his *Pietà* sculpture in Florence, Italy

1558

Elizabeth I is crowned in England, beginning a 45-year reign as queen

WORLD EVENTS

1560

Becomes regent after death of Francois II; new king, 10-year-old Charles IX, is too young to rule

1562

Forces through the Edict of January, allowing Huguenots to worship outside city gates; Guise attacks Huguenots at the Massacre of Vassy

1563

Steps down as regent; organizes Grand Progress for King Charles IX

1560

1564

Poet and playwright William Shakespeare is born

1561

Tulips are introduced in Europe from the Near East

DE MEDICI'S LIFE

1576

King Henri III signs the Peace of Monsieur, putting Protestants and Catholics on equal footing in France

1572

Failed assassination of Admiral Coligny leads to the St. Bartholomew's Day Massacre

1574

Charles IX dies, and Henri III becomes king of France

1570

1570

The potato is introduced to Europe from South America

1576

English navigator Martin Frobisher, on his search for the Northwest Passage, enters the Canadian bay that now bears his name

WORLD EVENTS

1578

Embarks on a peace
mission throughout
France

1589

Dies on January 5 at
age 69; Valois dynasty
comes to an end with
the death of Henri III

1590

1589

Galileo Galilei
becomes professor
of mathematics at
University of Pisa

1577

Francis Drake sails
around the world by
way of Cape Horn

DATE OF BIRTH: April 13, 1519

BIRTHPLACE: Florence, Italy

FATHER: Lorenzo de Medici, Duke of Urbino (1482–1519)

MOTHER: Madeleine de la Tour d'Auvergne (1502–1519)

SPOUSE: Henri II, king of France (1519-1559)

DATE OF MARRIAGE: October 28, 1533

CHILDREN: Francois (Francois II) (1544-1560)
Elisabeth (1545-1568)
Claude (1547-1575)
Louis (1549)
Charles (Charles IX) (1550-1574)
Edouard-Alexandre (Henri III) (1551-1589)
Marguerite (Margot) (1553-1615)
Francois-Hercules (1555-1584)
Victoire (1556)
Jeanne (1556)

DATE OF DEATH: January 5, 1589

PLACE OF BURIAL: Saint Sauveur; then Saint-Denis

Further Reading

Davis, Thomas J., and Martin Marty. *John Calvin.* Broomall, Pa.: Chelsea House, 2004.

Greenblatt, Marian. *Lorenzo de Medici and Renaissance Italy.* Tarrytown, N.Y.: Benchmark Books, 2002.

Hinds, Kathryn. *The Church: Life in the Renaissance.* Tarrytown, N.Y.: Benchmark Books, 2003.

Howarth, Susan. *Renaissance People.* Brookfield, Conn.: Millbrook Press, 1992.

Knecht, R. J. *Catherine dé Medici.* New York: Longman, 1998.

MacDonald, Fiona. *The Reformation.* Chicago: Raintree, 2002.

Stepanek, Sally. *Mary Queen of Scots.* Broomall, Pa.: Chelsea House, 1987.

Look for more Signature Lives
books about this era:

Desiderius Erasmus: *Writer and Christian Humanist*
ISBN 0-7565-1584-X

Martin Luther: *Father of the Reformation*
ISBN 0-7565-1593-9

Pope Leo X: *Opponent of the Reformation*
ISBN 0-7565-1594-7

William Tyndale: *Bible Translator and Martyr*
ISBN 0-7565-1599-8

On the Web

For more information on *Catherine de Medici*, use FactHound.

1. Go to *www.facthound.com*
2. Type in a search word related to this book or this book ID: 0756515815
3. Click on the *Fetch It* button.

FactHound will fetch the best Web sites for you.

Historic Sites

Huguenot Historical Society
18 Broadhead Ave.
New Paltz, NY 12561
845/255-1660
Exhibits, including historic homes, explain the cultural, religious, and political heritage of the Huguenot community in the United States.

The Metropolitan Museum of Art
1000 Fifth Ave.
New York, NY 10028
212/535-7710
Art and artifacts of the Reformation era are on display.

assassination
the murder of a well-known person

cardinal
a Catholic official ranking just below the pope

dauphin
the crown prince, or heir to the throne, of France

dowry
money, goods, or land a woman brings to her
husband when they marry

edict
a document announcing a law

embalmed
treated with chemicals after death to slow decay
of body tissues

fanatical
having wild enthusiasm about a belief, cause,
or interest

fistula
a passage from a source of pus to an opening on
the body's surface

heresy
the act of denying the established beliefs of
a religion

list
arena for jousting

mercenaries
soldiers who are paid to fight a foreign army

regent
one who rules a country in the absence of
or during the youth of a king or queen

Chapter 1

Page 11, line 9: Leonie Frieda. *Catherine de Medici: A Biography.* London: Weidenfeld & Nicolson, 2003, p. 266.

Chapter 2

Page 19, line 13: R. J. Knecht. *Catherine Dé Medici: Profiles in Power.* London: Addison Wesley Longman, 1998, p. 6.

Page 22, line 4: Mark Strage. *Women of Power: The Life and Times of Catherine dé Medici.* New York: Harcourt Brace Jovanovich, 1976, p. 21.

Page 25, line 18: Ibid., p. 20.

Chapter 3

Page 34, line 10: *Catherine Dé Medici: Profiles in Power,* p. 28.

Page 35, line 10: *Women of Power: The Life and Times of Catherine dé Medici,* p. 58.

Page 36, line 18: Ibid., p. 52.

Page 39, line 1: Ibid., p. 61.

Page 41, line 14: *Catherine de Medici: A Biography,* p. 131.

Chapter 4

Page 43, line 8: Edith Sichel. *Catherine dé Medici and the French Reformation.* London: Archibald Constable & Company, Ltd., 1905, p. 40.

Page 44, line 10: Ibid.

Page 53, line 20: *Catherine de Medici: A Biography,* p. 3.

Page 55, line 3: Irene Mahoney. *Madame Catherine.* New York: Coward, McCann & Geoghegan, Inc., 1975, p. 48.

Chapter 5

Page 57, line 5: *Women of Power: The Life and Times of Catherine dé Medici,* p. 116.

Page 59, line 24: *Catherine dé Medici and the French Reformation,* p. 106.

Page 60, line 21: *Women of Power: The Life and Times of Catherine dé Medici,* p. 128.

Chapter 6

Page 65, line 1: *Madame Catherine,* p. 88.

Page 67, line 1: *Catherine Dé Medici: Profiles in Power,* p. 88.

Page 68, line 8: *Madame Catherine,* p. 93.

Page 69, line 18: *Catherine de Medici: A Biography,* p. 168.

Page 70, line 4: *Women of Power: The Life and Times of Catherine dé Medici,* p. 146.

Chapter 7

Page 81, line 6: Ibid.

Page 81, line 25: *Catherine de Medici: A Biography*, p. 270.

Page 83, line 18: Ibid., p. 277.

Chapter 8

Page 88, line 21: Ibid., p. 327.

Page 89, line 1: Ibid., p. 328.

Page 93, line 20: *Catherine Dé Medici: Profiles in Power*, p. 266.

Page 93, line 23: Ibid., p. 267.

Frieda, Leonie. *Catherine de Medici: A Biography*. London: Weidenfeld & Nicolson, 2003.

Knecht, R. J. *Catherine Dé Medici: Profiles in Power*. London: Addison Wesley Longman, 1998.

Mahoney, Irene. *Madame Catherine*. New York: Coward, McCann & Geoghegan, Inc., 1975.

Sichel, Edith. *Catherine dé Medici and the French Reformation*. London: Archibald Constable & Company, Ltd., 1905.

Strage, Mark. *Women of Power: The Life and Times of Catherine dé Medici*. New York: Harcourt Brace Jovanovich, 1976.

Barbara A. Somervill has been writing for more than 30 years. She has written newspaper and magazine articles, video scripts, and books for children. She enjoys writing about science and investigating people's lives for biographies. She is an avid reader and traveler. Ms. Somervill lives with her husband in South Carolina.

Image Credits